noodles

noodles

Great recipe ideas with a classic ingredient

>> in 60 ways

mc Marshall Cavendish Cuisine

The publisher wishes to thank Lim's Art and Living Pte Ltd for the loan and use of their tableware.

Design: Bernard Go Kwang Meng
Photography: Jambu Studio

Published by Marshall Cavendish Cuisine
An imprint of Marshall Cavendish International
1 New Industrial Road, Singapore 536196

Other Marshall Cavendish Offices:
Marshall Cavendish Ltd. 119 Wardour Street, London W1F 0UW, UK · Marshall Cavendish Corporation. 99 White Plains Road, Tarrytown NY 10591-9001, USA · Marshall Cavendish International (Thailand) Co Ltd. 253 Asoke, 12th Flr, Sukhumvit 21 Road, Klongtoey Nua, Wattana, Bangkok 10110, Thailand · Marshall Cavendish (Malaysia) Sdn Bhd, Times Subang, Lot 46, Subang Hi-Tech Industrial Park, Batu Tiga, 40000 Shah Alam, Selangor Darul Ehsan, Malaysia

Marshall Cavendish is a trademark of Times Publishing Limited

National Library Board Singapore Cataloguing in Publication Data

Noodles in 60 ways. – Singapore :- Marshall Cavendish Cuisine,- c2006.
p. cm. – (In 60 ways)
ISBN-13 : 978-981-261-291-5
ISBN-10 : 981-261-291-2

1. Cookery (Pasta) I. Title: Noodles in sixty ways II. Series: In 60 ways

TX809.N65
641.822 -- dc22   SLS2006018804

Printed in Singapore by Times Graphics Pte Ltd

contents ≫

introduction »

Defining noodles can be an arduous task. Strictly speaking, noodles are long strips of pasta or of a similar flour paste. In Asia, however, the term noodles is used as a broad reference to all sorts of noodles and pasta shapes, regardless of a ribbonlike nature. An elbow macaroni, for example, would be classified as a noodle in Asia, but would not in the narrow definition of noodles. Whatever the definition, one fact remains: due to its long shelf life and its economic, filling and nutritious nature, noodles are a large part of the world's diet.

Who invented noodles? Despite the claims of the Arabs and the Italians, the earliest known historical records indicate that the Chinese have been slurping up noodles for over 4,000 years. It is no surprise then that noodles are significant in the Chinese culture, as its long slender form symbolises longevity and is therefore served at the end of birthday meals.

Noodles are enjoyed in various forms in China. Cooked Chinese noodles can divided into two broad categories: "lo mein" and "chow mein". The former are boiled noodles that are served with a hot broth and condiments and the latter are noodles that have been stir-fried. Chinese noodles are also categorised according to its base ingredients—egg, wheat and rice flour noodles.

In Japan, locals huddle elbow-to-elbow over steamy bowls of noodles in ramen and udon noodle shops. A typical Japanese bowl of noodles, both hot and cold forms, have four essential elements: noodles, broth or sauce, toppings and garnishes. Slurping your noodles noisily in Japan is perfectly acceptable and encouraged as it helps to cool down your noodles before eating.

Pasta, the quintessence of Italian cooking, is made from semolina flour, eggs, salt and water or milk. Pasta comes in a spectrum of shapes and flavours that are designed to accommodate different types of sauces. Thin and delicate pasta noodles such as Angel Hair or *Capelli d'Angelo* are ideal for light or oil-based sauces while broader pasta noodles such as fettucine, which have a larger surface area, are better for slurping up creamier sauces.

The noodles used in this book—rice noodles, egg noodles, glass (transparent) noodles, buckwheat noodles and pastas—follow the narrower definition of noodles and are by no means exhaustive of all the varieties of noodles available today.

Storing Noodles

If stored unopened or in an airtight container with its drying agent in a cool dry place, dried noodles will last indefinitely, but should be consumed within 6–8 months. Fresh pasta and noodles, stored in an airtight container, will keep for up to 2–3 days in the refrigerator and up to a month in the freezer.

Cooking Noodles: The Craft of It

The perfect pasta is cooked to the point of "al dente", which literally translates from Italian as "to the tooth". At this point, the noodle is just cooked through with a slight firmness when eaten. Cooking good noodles is relatively easy once you know the basics. As a rule of thumb, portion 75 g (2^1/$_2$ oz) of dried noodles or 100 g (3^1/$_2$ oz) of fresh noodles per person. Boil 450 g (1 lb) of noodles in 4 litres (16 cups / 6^2/$_5$ pints) of water with 2 Tbsp of salt. Add noodles to the water when it comes to a vigorous boil then stir occasionally to prevent the noodles from clumping. Once the water returns to the boil, start timing your cooking time and lift occasionally to check for doneness. The craft of making good noodles is in precise timing. Dried noodles differ between manufacturers and brands so the best guide when cooking dried noodles is to follow the cooking time as directed on the package while fresh noodles only require about 3 minutes.

cold noodles & salads

soba, mango and cucumber salad

Make this cheerful coloured cold salad on a hot day. The sweetness of the mango and the cool crunchiness of the cucumber will be refreshing.

Serves 6

Ingredients

Dried soba	180 g (6 oz)
Tomatoes	2, peeled and cut into small cubes
Cucumber	½, julienned
Mango	1, halved, pitted and thinly sliced
Chopped fresh basil	3 Tbsp
Chopped fresh mint	3 Tbsp
Salted peanuts	100 g (3½ oz), chopped
Limes	2, cut into wedges

Dressing

Rice vinegar	90 ml (3 fl oz / ⅜ cup)
Sugar	2 Tbsp
Salt	½ tsp
Garlic	1 clove, peeled and chopped
Bird's eye chilli	1, seeded and chopped
Lime	2, grated for zest + squeezed for 1½ Tbsp juice
Sesame oil	1 Tbsp

Method

- Prepare dressing. Add vinegar, sugar, and salt to a small saucepan. Warm over medium heat, stirring occasionally, for 1 minute or until sugar dissolves. Stir in garlic and chilli. Remove from heat and set aside to cool. Mix in lime zest and juice and sesame oil.

- Bring a pot of salted water to the boil. Add soba and cook until tender but still firm to the bite, stirring occasionally. Drain well. Rinse under cold water and drain well. Transfer soba to large bowl.

- Add dressing to soba, toss and mix evenly.

- Add cucumber, mango, basil and mint to soba and toss well. Arrange salad on a platter. Sprinkle with chopped peanuts and serve with lime wedges.

spicy pasta salad

This salad dressing is creamy and picante, making this salad a refreshing and spicy first course. Serve with hot crusty bread to enjoy as a light lunch.

Serves 4–6

Ingredients

Angel hair	450 g (1 lb)
Olive oil	1½ Tbsp
Sun-dried tomatoes	4, cut into bite-sized pieces
Corn kernels	350 g (12 oz)
Green apples	3, large, cored and cut into sticks
Red onion	½, large, peeled and sliced
Chopped coriander leaves (cilantro)	50 g (2 oz) + extra for garnishing
Salt	to taste
Ground black pepper	to taste

Salad Dressing

Mayonnaise	125 ml (4 fl oz / ½ cup)
Dijon mustard	2 Tbsp
Lime juice	2 Tbsp
Chilli powder	1¼ tsp
Ground cumin	1¼ tsp

Method

- Prepare salad dressing. Combine all ingredients in a small bowl. Mix well and set aside.

- Bring a pot of salted water to the boil. Add angel hair and cook until al dente. Drain well. Rinse with cold water and drain again. Transfer pasta to a salad bowl.

- Add olive oil to pasta, mix and coat evenly. Add tomatoes, corn, apples, onion and coriander and toss well. Season to taste with salt and pepper.

- Drizzle dressing on salad. Garnish with coriander and serve immediately.

chinese cold noodles with peanut sauce

Chinese Cold Noodles with Peanut Sauce is a perfect balance of sweet, savoury and spicy flavours.

Serves 4

Ingredients

Thick rice vermicelli	450 g (1 lb)
Sesame oil	2 Tbsp
Cucumber	½, medium, seeded, and julienned
Roasted peanuts	85 g (3 oz), chopped
Spring onions (scallions)	2, thinly sliced
Carrot	1, julienned and soaked in iced water

Dressing

Peanut butter	100 g (3½ oz)
Water	60 ml (2 fl oz / ¼ cup)
Light soy sauce	3 Tbsp
Dark soy sauce	90 ml (3 fl oz / ⅜ cup)
Roasted white sesame seeds	2 Tbsp
Sesame oil	125 ml (4 fl oz / ½ cup)
Chinese cooking wine (*hua tiao*)	2 Tbsp
Rice vinegar	1½ Tbsp
Honey	60 ml (2 fl oz / ¼ cup)
Garlic	4 cloves, peeled and finely chopped
Chopped ginger	2 tsp
Hot water	125 ml (4 fl oz / ½ cup)

Method

- Bring a large pot of water to the boil. Add noodles and cook until barely tender and still firm. Drain and plunge into cold water. Drain well and toss noodles with sesame oil and transfer to a serving dish.

- Prepare dressing. Combine all ingredients except hot water in a blender (food processor) until smooth. Add hot water and blend until the consistency of whipping cream.

- Top noodles with cucumber, peanuts, spring onions, and carrot. Serve noodles at room temperature with sauce on the side.

cold soba

Cold soba is a popular dish Japanese dish that is particularly enjoyed in the summer as it is cool and refreshing.

Serves 4

Ingredients

Dried soba	250 g (9 oz)
Nori (seaweed)	1 sheet, cut into thin strips
Spring onions (scallions)	3, chopped

Dipping Sauce

Dashi stock	300 ml (10 fl oz / 1¼ cups)
Light soy sauce	125 ml (4 fl oz / ½ cup)
Mirin	60 ml (2 fl oz / ⅓ cup)
Sake	1 Tbsp
Sugar	1 tsp

Method

- Prepare dipping sauce. Combine ingredients for dipping sauce in a saucepan. Heat mixture to cook off alcohol, remove from heat and set aside to cool. Chill in refrigerator.

- Bring a pot of salted water to boil. Add soba and cook for 3–5 minutes or until just tender. Drain and plunge into an ice bath and leave to chill for one minute. Drain well and transfer to serving dish.

- Garnish soba with nori and spring onions and serve with dipping sauce on the side.

An ice bath is a mixture of iced water that is used to rapidly chill ingredients to stop the cooking process.

chilli udon chicken salad

This is a scrumptious combination of udon, crispy chicken pieces and sweet and spicy chilli sauce. Serve with chilled beer.

Serves 2

Ingredients

Udon	150 g (5 oz)
Thai chilli sauce	60 ml (2 fl oz / ¼ cup)
Bean sprouts	55 g (2 oz), washed and trimmed
Cooking oil for deep-frying	
Chicken breast fillets	2, cubed
Corn flour (cornstarch)	100 g (3½ oz)
Egg white	1, lightly beaten
Spring onions (scallions)	2, thinly sliced
Roasted white sesame seeds	1 tsp

Method

- Bring a pot of salted water to the boil. Add udon and cook for 3 minutes. Drain and transfer to a bowl. Add 2 Tbsp chilli sauce and bean sprouts, mix well and set aside.

- Heat oil for deep-frying. Toss chicken pieces in corn flour then coat with egg white. Gently lower chicken pieces into hot oil. Deep-fry until crisp and golden brown. Drain well.

- Divide noodles and chicken pieces among 2 individual serving bowls. Drizzle with remaining chilli sauce. Garnish with spring onions and sesame seeds and serve immediately.

crispy noodle caesar salad

The use of crispy noodles instead of coutons gives the classic Caesar Salad an oriental twist. Serve as an appetiser or as an accompaniment to roasted meat dishes.

Serves 4

Ingredients

Cooking oil for deep-frying	
Thin yellow egg noodles	125 g (4$\frac{1}{2}$ oz), cut into shorter lengths
Bacon	3 slices, cut into 2.5-cm (1-in) pieces
Chicken breast fillets	750 g (1 lb 10 oz), halved
Baby cos lettuce	1, cut into 2.5-cm (1-in) wide strips
Eggs	3, hard-boiled, peeled and quartered
Caesar salad dressing	85 ml (2$\frac{1}{2}$ fl oz / $\frac{1}{3}$ cup)

Method

- Heat oil for deep-frying and gently in lower egg noodles. Deep-fry until golden brown. Drain well and set aside. Reserve 1 Tbsp oil.

- Heat reserved oil in a non-stick frying pan over medium-high heat. Add bacon and fry for 3–4 minutes or until crisp. Drain and set aside.

- In the same pan, add half the chicken. Cook for 3 minutes each side or until golden brown and cooked through. Drain, set aside and allow to cool. Repeat with remaining chicken. Thinly slice chicken and transfer to a salad bowl.

- Add lettuce leaves to the salad bowl, toss and mix well. Crumble in bacon and crispy noodles and top with eggs.

- Drizzle dressing over salad and serve immediately.

thai glass noodle salad

This classic Thai salad is known as Yum Woon Sen *has a tangy sauce and makes a good salad to serve as part of a Thai meal.*

Serves 2

Ingredients

Cooking oil	2 Tbsp
Minced pork	200 g (7 oz)
Bird's eye chilli	1, seeded and chopped
Bean sprouts	300 g (10½ oz), chopped
Spring onions (scallions)	3, finely chopped
Glass (transparent) noodle	200 g (7 oz), cut into 5-cm (2-in) length then soaked to soften
Chopped roasted peanuts	2 Tbsp
Coriander leaves (cilantro)	1 sprig

Sauce

Light soy sauce	2 Tbsp
Thai fish sauce	2 Tbsp
Sweet chilli sauce	2 Tbsp
Light brown sugar	1 Tbsp
Rice vinegar	2 Tbsp

Method

- Prepare sauce. Combine all sauce ingredients in a bowl and set aside.

- Heat oil in a wok. Add pork and fry until it browns, about 2–3 minutes. Add chopped chilli, bean sprouts and spring onions and stir-fry for 1 minute.

- Add noodles and sauce. Toss ingredients together and remove from heat. Transfer to a serving plate, garnish with peanuts and coriander and serve immediately.

cold sesame noodles

With the exception of boiling the dried soba, this refreshing bowl of noodles does not require any cooking.

Serves 6

Ingredients

Dried soba	250 g (9 oz)
Honey	60 ml (2 fl oz / $\frac{1}{4}$ cup)
Rice vinegar	60 ml (2 fl oz / $\frac{1}{4}$ cup)
Light soy sauce	60 ml (2 fl oz / $\frac{1}{4}$ cup)
Sesame oil	2 Tbsp
Cos lettuce	$\frac{1}{2}$ head, roughly chopped
Cucumber	1, large, seeded and cut into long strips
Carrot	1, cut into long strips
Ham	225 g (8 oz)
Chopped coriander leaves (cilantro)	6 sprigs
Roasted white sesame seeds	1 Tbsp

Method

- Bring a saucepan of water to the boil over high heat. Add soba and cook, stirring occasionally, for 3–5 minutes or until just tender. Drain, rinse under cold water to cool, and drain again.

- Combine honey, vinegar, soy sauce and oil. Mix well and chill in refrigerator for 30 minutes.

- Place soba in a serving dish and mix with cos lettuce, cucumber, carrot, ham and coriander. Pour chilled dressing over salad. Sprinkle with sesame seeds and serve.

vietnamese noodle salad with beef skewers

Known also as Bun Cha, Vietnamese Noodle Salad is an everyday Vietnamese dish that is enjoyed with savoury barbecued beef or pork.

Serves 4

Ingredients

Rice vinegar	90 ml (3 fl oz / $^3/_8$ cup)
Thai fish sauce	60 ml (2 fl oz / $^1/_4$ cup)
Sugar	1 Tbsp
Beef	600 g (14 oz), trimmed of excess fat and cut into strips
Glass (transparent) noodles	200 g (7 oz)
Carrot	1, cut into thin sticks
Red chilli	1, thinly sliced
Mint leaves	30 g (1 oz)
Fresh coriander leaves (cilantro)	45 g (1$^1/_2$ oz)

Method

- Soak 12 wooden skewers in cold water for 20 minutes.

- Mix 2 Tbsp vinegar with 1 Tbsp fish sauce and sugar in a bowl. Add beef and toss to coat. Cover and refrigerate for 10 minutes.

- Meanwhile, place noodles and carrot in a bowl and pour boiling water over. Let stand for a few minutes to soften, then drain.

- Combine noodles with chilli, mint, coriander and remaining fish sauce and vinegar. Toss and mix well. Transfer to a serving dish.

- Heat a lightly oiled grill over medium heat. While heating up, thread beef strips onto skewers. Grill or barbecue for 3–5 minutes until cooked through. Serve immediately with noodles.

vegetarian

linguine with garlic, olive oil and chillies

Pasta with garlic, olive oil and chillies is known as Aglio Olio e Peperoncino *in Italian. For those who prefer a milder flavour, seed the chillies before adding them to the sauce. Serve with crusty bread.*

Serves 4–6

Ingredients

Linguine	450 g (1 lb)
Olive oil	125 ml (4 fl oz / ½ cup)
Garlic	4 cloves, peeled and sliced
Red chillies	2, sliced
Chopped parsley leaves	4 Tbsp
Salt	a pinch
Ground black pepper	2 tsp

Method

- Bring a pot of salted water to the boil. Add linguine and cook until al dente. Drain well, transfer to a large serving dish and keep warm.
- In a small saucepan, heat oil over moderate heat. Add all ingredients and fry, stirring constantly, for 3 minutes or until garlic begins to turn golden.
- Reduce heat to low and continue cooking for a further 3 minutes, take care not to let garlic burn. Remove pan from heat.
- Pour flavoured oil over linguine, toss and mix well. Serve immediately.

clear glass noodle soup

This clear vegetable-based broth is healthy, light and nourishing.
Serves 4

Ingredients

Cucumber	½, coarsely chopped
Garlic	2 cloves, peeled and halved
Cabbage	90 g (3 oz), cored and chopped
Water	1.25 litres (40 fl oz / 5 cups)
Dried lily buds	15 g (½ oz), soaked to soften
Dried Chinese mushrooms	1, soaked to soften, stems discarded and sliced, reserve liquid
Glass (transparent) noodles	115 g (4 oz)
Thai fish sauce	2 Tbsp
Light brown sugar	1 Tbsp
Soft bean curd	90 g (3 oz), diced
Fresh coriander leaves (cilantro)	1 sprig

Method

- Combine cucumber, garlic and cabbage in a blender (processor) until a smooth paste is formed.

- Add paste and water in a pot. Bring liquid to the boil, then reduce heat to a simmer and cook for 2 minutes, stirring occasionally. Strain, discard residue and return liquid to the pot.

- Bring liquid to simmering point. Add lily buds, mushrooms, noodles, fish sauce and sugar, stir and cook for 5 minutes or until noodles are soft.

- Divide bean curd among 4 serving bowls. Ladle soup into bowls, garnish with coriander and serve immediately.

indian-styled fried noodles

This Singaporean noodle dish was invented by Indian hawkers and combines Chinese, Indian and Western ingredients.

Serves 4

Ingredients

Cooking oil	125 ml (4 fl oz / ½ cup)
Firm bean curd	1, cut into bite-sized pieces
Red onion	1, medium, peeled and chopped
Thick yellow egg noodles	500 g (1 lb 1½ oz), blanched
Chives (*kucai*) or spring onions (scallions)	2, sliced into 2.5-cm (1-in) lengths
Curry leaves	1 sprig
Tomato sauce	2 Tbsp
Chilli sauce	1 Tbsp
Light soy sauce	2 tsp
Eggs	2, lightly beaten
Potato	1, boiled, peeled and cut into small dice
Green chilli	1, sliced

Method

- Heat oil in wok and fry bean curd until golden brown. Drain and set aside.

- In the same wok, fry onion for 2–3 minutes or until soft. Add noodles, chives, curry leaves and sauces. Cook over low heat, stirring gently, for 3–4 minutes.

- Pour over beaten egg and leave to set for about 45 seconds before stirring to mix with noodles. Add potato and bean curd, stir to mix and cook for another 30 seconds.

- Transfer to a serving dish. Garnish with green chilli and serve hot.

noodles with mushrooms

This dish is easy to prepare and is very good served with a meat casseroles.

Serves 6

Ingredients

Cooked spinach fettucine	450 g (1 lb)
Melted butter	60 ml (2 fl oz / $1/4$ cup)
White button mushrooms	110 g (4 oz), caps wiped and sliced
Dried basil	$1/4$ tsp
Dried marjoram	$1/4$ tsp
Salt	$1/2$ tsp
Ground black pepper	$1/2$ tsp

Method

- Preheat oven to 170°C (325°F).
- Combine all ingredients in a baking dish. Toss and mix well.
- Cover baking dish with aluminium foil and bake for 20 minutes.
- Remove from oven, transfer to a serving dish and serve immediately.

linguine with spicy coriander sauce

This zingy tasting pasta is coated with a light chilli and coriander flavoured olive oil. Serve as a first course for an Italian meal.

Serves 4

Ingredients

Linguine	400 g (14 oz)
Olive oil	60 ml (2 fl oz / $\frac{1}{4}$ cup)
Onion	1, peeled and minced
Garlic	1 clove, peeled and minced
Courgette (zucchini)	1, quartered
Vegetable stock	180 ml (6 fl oz / $\frac{3}{4}$ cup)
Chopped coriander leaves (cilantro)	1 Tbsp
Salt	1 tsp
Ground black pepper	1 tsp
Dried chilli flakes	1 tsp
Parmesan cheese (optional)	

Method

• Bring a pot of salted water to the boil. Add linguine and cook until al dente. Drain, transfer to a mixing bowl and keep warm.

• Heat oil in a large frying pan over medium heat. Sauté onion and garlic for 5 minutes or until onion is soft and translucent but not brown.

• Add courgette, stock, coriander, salt, pepper and chilli flakes and cook for 10 minutes, stirring occasionally. Remove from heat and add to linguine. Toss and mix well.

• Transfer to 4 serving plates or bowls and serve immediately with freshly grated Parmesan cheese, if desired.

pad thai with tofu

Pad Thai with Tofu, is an economical and scumptious noodle dish that is sold by food hawkers in Thailand.

Serves 4

Ingredients

Cooking oil	60 ml (2 fl oz / ¼ cup)
Firm bean curd	300 g (10 oz), cubed
Shallots	5, peeled and thinly sliced
Garlic	3 cloves, peeled and finely chopped
Carrot	1, peeled, halved lengthways and thinly sliced diagonally
Red capsicum (bell pepper)	1, white pith removed and thinly sliced
Eggs	2, lightly whisked
Rice sticks	250 g (9 oz), soaked in water to soften and drained
Bean sprouts	100 g (3½ oz)
Chinese cabbage	¼ head, cored and shredded
Fresh coriander leaves (cilantro)	6 sprigs
Unsalted peanuts	2 Tbsp, crushed
Lime	1, cut into wedges

Sauce

Sweet soy sauce	1½ Tbsp
Tamarind concentrate	1 Tbsp
Lime juice	1 Tbsp
Chopped palm sugar	2 tsp

Method

- Prepare sauce. Combine all ingredients in a bowl. Mix well and set aside.

- Heat 2 Tbsp oil in a wok over medium-high heat until just smoking. Add half the bean curd and gently stir-fry for 2 minutes or until golden brown. Drain well. Repeat process with remaining bean curd.

- Heat remaining oil in the same wok over medium heat until just smoking. Add shallots and garlic and stir-fry for 2 minutes or until shallots soften.

- Add carrot and capsicum, and stir-fry for 2 minutes or until carrot is tender.

- Make a well in the centre of mixture. Pour eggs into the well and stir-fry until partially cooked. Add rice sticks and stir-fry until well combined.

- Add sauce, bean curd, bean sprouts, cabbage, coriander, and stir-fry until well combined. Remove from heat.

- Divide noodles among 4 serving plates and sprinkle with peanuts. Serve immediately with lime wedges.

lemony angel hair

This comforting pasta sauce is made with cream, lemon, parsley and Parmesan cheese.

Serves 4

Ingredients

Angel hair	300 g (10½ oz)
Butter	3 Tbsp
Heavy (double) cream	180 ml (6 fl oz / ¾ cup)
Lemons	3, grated for zest and squeezed for 60 ml (2 fl oz / ¼ cup) juice
Salt	¾ tsp
Chopped parsley leaves	75 g (2½ oz)
Grated Parmesan cheese	50 g (2 oz)

Method

- Bring a pot of salted water to the boil. Add angel hair and cook until al dente.
- Meanwhile, heat butter and cream in a saucepan over low heat until butter is melted. Stir in lemon zest and juice, and salt. Remove pan from heat.
- Drain pasta and transfer to a large bowl. Add sauce and parsley, toss and mix well.
- Dish into 4 serving bowls, top with Parmesan cheese and serve immediately.

linguine arrabiata

Arrabiata means spicy hot in Italian. This hot and spicy pasta dish combines tomatoes, garlic and chilli flakes. Add more chilli flakes until desired hotness or go easy on the chilli flakes if you are a chilli beginner.

Serves 2

Ingredients

Linguine	200 g (7 oz)
Olive oil	2 tsp
Garlic	2 cloves, peeled and finely chopped
Canned chopped tomatoes	200 g (7 oz), drained
Lemon	1; $^1/_2$ grated for zest + $^1/_2$ sliced
Dried chilli flakes	$^1/_2$ tsp
Balsamic vinegar	2 tsp
Sugar	1 tsp
Salt	to taste
Ground black pepper	to taste
Chopped fresh parsley	2 tsp

Method

- Bring a pot of salted water to the boil. Add linguine and cook until al dente.

- Meanwhile, heat oil in a medium saucepan. Sauté garlic and chopped tomatoes until warmed through. Add lemon zest, chilli flakes, vinegar and sugar. Simmer for 3–4 minutes.

- Drain linguine and add to saucepan. Season with salt and pepper to taste. Toss and coat well.

- Transfer to a serving dish. Sprinkle chopped parsley, garnish as desired and serve with lemon slices.

pasta with avocado, ginger, pine nuts and coriander

When serving this incredibly refreshing pasta, it is essential that the linguine, roasted pine nuts and serving plates are all piping hot. The coriander should also be handpicked just before serving to keep the herb as fresh as possible.

Serves 2

Ingredients

Linguine	200 g (7 oz)
Avocado	1, small, halved and stoned
Lemon	1, squeezed for juice
Ginger	1-cm (1/2-in) knob, peeled and finely chopped
Extra virgin olive oil	85 ml (2 1/2 fl oz / 1/3 cup)
Roasted pine nuts	2 Tbsp
Fresh coriander leaves (cilantro)	3 sprigs
Salt	to taste
Ground black pepper	to taste

Method

- Bring a pot of salted water to the boil. When water is boiling, add linguine and cook until al dente.
- Meanwhile, peel and chop avocado flesh into chunks and pour over 1 Tbsp lemon juice to prevent browning.
- Combine ginger and 1 Tbsp olive oil. Drain and toss hot pasta with ginger oil.
- Add pine nuts, remaining olive oil, avocado, remaining lemon juice and coriander. Season with salt and pepper to taste and serve immediately.

seafood

squid and spinach pasta

This dish consists of iron-rich spinach and crispy squid rings, making it both nutritious and delicious.

Serves 3

Ingredients

Linguine	220 g (8 oz)
Olive oil	2 tsp
Shiitake mushrooms	175 g (6 oz), caps wiped and sliced
Spinach leaves	175 g (6 oz)
Cooking oil for deep-frying	
Squid rings	110 g (4 oz)
Salt	to taste
Ground black pepper	to taste
Self-raising flour	200 g (7 oz)

Method

- Bring a pot of salted water to the boil. Add linguine and cook until al dente. Drain and transfer to a large glass bowl and keep warm.

- Heat oil in a large non-stick frying pan and sauté mushrooms for 2 minutes. Stir in half the spinach. Cook for another 2 minutes.

- Remove pan from heat and stir mushrooms and spinach into cooked pasta. Stir in remaining uncooked spinach leaves and mix well. Set aside.

- Season squid rings with salt and pepper. Coat squid rings evenly with flour.

- Heat oil for deep-frying. Deep-fry squid rings for 2–3 minutes or until crisp and golden. Drain well.

- Transfer pasta to serving plates and top with crispy squid. Serve immediately.

fried hokkien noodles

Although relatively time consuming, the process of making the prawn stock is important as it forms the basis of this dish. Store bought seafood stock cubes can be used as a substitute, but will not have the richness of the homemade prawn stock.

Serves 4

Ingredients

Thick yellow egg noodles	500 g (1 lb 1½ oz)
Cooking oil	3 Tbsp
Prawns (shrimps)	250 g (8 oz), peeled, reserve shells and heads
Chicken stock	250 ml (8 fl oz / 1 cup)
Squid rings	100 g (3½ oz)
Garlic	8–10 cloves, peeled and pounded
Eggs	2, lightly beaten
Bean sprouts	250 g (8 oz), tailed
Spring onions (scallions)	2, cut into 5-cm (2-in) lengths
Salt	to taste
Ground black pepper	to taste

Method

- Soak noodles in boiling water for 1 minute. Drain and set aside.

- Heat 1 Tbsp oil in a saucepan. Fry prawn shells and heads, stirring constantly for 1 minute. Add stock and bring to the boil. Cover pan and simmer for 5 minutes. Strain, discard shells and heads and return stock to the saucepan.

- Add prawns and squid rings and boil until cooked. Strain and set stock, prawns and squid rings aside.

- Heat remaining oil in a wok over medium heat. Add garlic and fry until golden to flavour the oil. Discard garlic.

- Increase heat to high. When oil is really hot, pour in beaten eggs and stir constantly for 1 minute.

- Add noodles, cooked prawns and squid rings, bean sprouts, spring onions and 125 ml (4 fl oz / ½ cup) stock and cook for 1 minute. Season to taste with salt and pepper.

- Transfer to a serving dish and serve immediately.

linguine alle vongole

Linguine alle Vongole is a delicious pasta dish from Naples, Italy. If clams are unavailable, cockles or mussels may be substituted.

Makes 4–6 servings

Ingredients

Butter	3 Tbsp
Garlic	2 cloves, peeled and sliced
Onion	1, small, peeled and finely chopped
Canned peeled tomatoes	450 g (1 lb), drained
Salt	1/4 tsp
Ground white pepper	1/2 tsp
Dried basil	1/2 tsp
Little neck clams	450 g (1 lb)
Chopped fresh parsley	1 Tbsp
Cooked linguine	450 g (1 lb), drained and kept hot
Lemon	1, cut into wedges

Method

- Heat butter in a medium saucepan. When butter is hot, add garlic and onion. Fry, stirring occasionally for 5–7 minutes, or until onion is soft and translucent but not brown.

- Stir in tomatoes, salt, pepper and basil and bring mixture to the boil, stirring constantly. Reduce heat to low, cover pan and simmer, stirring occasionally, for a further 30 minutes.

- Add clams and parsley. Cover pan and cook for a further 5 minutes or until clams open. Discard clams that remain closed. Remove pan from heat.

- Place linguine in a large, deep serving dish and pour sauce over. Toss quickly until linguine is well coated with sauce.

- Transfer into individual serving plates and serve with lemon wedges.

char kway teow
(fried flat rice noodles)

Char Kway Teow is traditionally cooked with lard by hawkers in Singapore and Malaysia. Lard was used in the past as it made this dish tasty and a good source of energy for the coolies. This healthier version uses vegetable oil instead of lard.

Serves 6–8

Ingredients

Vegetable oil	3 Tbsp
Garlic	4 cloves, peeled and finely chopped
Red chillies	3; 2 pounded, 1 sliced
Chinese sausage (*Lup cheong*)	200 g (6½ oz), sliced
Prawns (shrimps)	375 g (12 oz), peeled with tails left intact
Light soy sauce	1 Tbsp
Dark soy sauce	1 Tbsp
Oyster sauce	2 tsp
Salt	½ tsp
Ground black pepper	to taste
Bean sprouts	250 g (8 oz)
Fresh flat rice noodles	1 kg (2 lb 3 oz), blanched

Method

- Heat oil in a wok. Fry garlic and chillies until garlic starts to turn golden. Increase heat, add Chinese sausage and stir-fry for another 2 minutes.
- Add prawns and stir-fry for another 2 minutes. Add sauces, salt, pepper and bean sprouts. Mix well and stir-fry for 2 minutes.
- Add noodles and stir-fry for 2–3 minutes or until noodles are well coated. Transfer to a serving dish and serve immediately.

linguine with tuna and tomato salsa

With the convenience of canned tuna, this healthy dish can be effortlessly put together in less than 15 minutes. Serve as a light lunch.

Serves 4

Ingredients

Linguine	300 g (13½ oz)
Canned tuna flakes	250 g (9 oz)

Salsa

Cherry tomatoes	250 g (9 oz), halved
Red onion	1, sliced
Chopped fresh parsley	5 Tbsp
Chopped fresh basil	5 Tbsp
Olive oil	3 Tbsp
Garlic	1 clove, peeled and minced
Salt	to taste
Ground black pepper	to taste

Method

- Prepare salsa. Combine all ingredients in a bowl and set aside.
- Bring a pot of salted water to the boil. Add linguine and cook until al dente. Drain and transfer to a large bowl.
- Add tuna flakes and salsa to pasta and mix well. Serve warm or at room temperature.

NOTE

As a variation, substitute canned salmon flakes for canned tuna flakes and chopped fresh dill for chopped fresh basil.

chilli rice noodles with fish cakes

These spicy fish cakes are a simple version of the Thai fish cakes that are enjoyed as everyday snacks in Thailand. Serve as a filling appetiser or a light lunch.

Serves 4

Ingredients

Rice sticks	200 g (7 oz)
White-fleshed fish fillet (cod or grouper)	500 g (1 lb 1½ oz), roughly chopped
Red chilli	1, chopped
Ginger	1-cm (½-in) knob, peeled and grated
Lemon grass	1 stalk, minced
Salt	½ tsp
Egg whites	2
Thai fish sauce	1 Tbsp
Chopped coriander leaves (cilantro)	3 Tbsp
Sping onion (scallion)	1, sliced
Cooking oil	60 ml (2 fl oz / ¼ cup)
Cucumbers	2, seeded and julienned

Dipping Sauce

White vinegar	250 ml (8 fl oz / 1 cup)
Sugar	50 g (2 oz)
Red chilli	1, large, chopped

Method

- Prepare dipping sauce. Place vinegar and sugar in a small saucepan over low heat. Stir until sugar is dissolved. Increase heat to high and boil for 10 minutes or until syrupy. Add chilli and set aside.

- Place rice sticks in a bowl and cover with boiling water. Soak for 15–20 minutes or until soft. Drain and keep warm.

- Combine fish, chilli, ginger, lemon grass, salt, egg whites and fish sauce in a blender (processor) until smooth. Transfer to a bowl and stir in coriander and spring onion. Divide mixture into 10 equal portions.

- Roll each portion of mixture into a ball then flatten into 9-cm (3½-in) diameter fish cakes. Make 10 fish cakes.

- Heat oil in a frying pan. Fry fish cakes for 3 minutes each side or until dark golden and cooked through. Drain well.

- Mix rice sticks and 2 Tbsp dipping sauce. Mix evenly.

- Transfer rice sticks into serving bowls. Top with cucumber and serve with fish cakes and dipping sauce.

stir-fried curry noodles

This dish is a great way to use up leftovers as you can substitute prawns with chicken, fish or squid and still cook a scumptious one-pot meal.

Serves 4

Ingredients

Thin yellow egg noodles	150 g (5 oz)
Cooking oil	1 Tbsp
Garlic	1 clove, peeled and crushed
Ginger	1-cm (1/2-in) knob, peeled and grated
Red chilli	1, small, seeded and chopped
Prawns (shrimps)	300 g (10 1/2 oz), medium, peeled, deveined, tails intact and cooked,
Peas	50 g (2 oz)
Spring onions (scallions)	2, finely chopped
Chicken stock	150 ml (5 fl oz / 5/8 cup)
Egg	1, lightly beaten
Chopped coriander leaves (cilantro)	2 Tbsp

Sauce

Light soy sauce	1 Tbsp
Chinese cooking wine (*hua tiao*)	1 Tbsp
Sugar	1 tsp
Mild curry powder	2 tsp

Method

- Place noodles in a large bowl. Pour over boiling water, soak for 2 minutes and drain.

- Prepare sauce. Combine all ingredients a small bowl. Mix well and set aside.

- Heat oil in a wok over high heat. Add garlic, ginger and chilli, stir-fry for 1 minute.

- Add prawns, peas, spring onions, noodles, stock and sauce and stir-fry for 1–2 minutes until heated through.

- Add egg, stir quickly to break up, then stir in coriander. Remove from heat.

- Transfer to a serving dish and serve hot.

udon with clam broth

When cooked, the clams sweeten the stock with their natural juices resulting in a rich tasting stock. Serve piping hot.

Serves 4

Ingredients

Cooking oil	1 Tbsp
Little neck clams	900 g (2 lb), cleaned
Lemon grass	6 stalks, sliced
Ginger	2.5-cm (1-in) knob, peeled and shredded
Red bird's eye chillies	2, sliced + extra for garnishing
Onion	1, peeled and sliced
Salt	to taste
Ground black pepper	to taste
Mirin	85 ml (2½ fl oz / ⅓ cup)
Chicken stock	1 litre (32 fl oz / 4 cups)
Udon	300 g (10½ oz)
Butter (optional)	1 Tbsp
Lemon juice	1 Tbsp

Method

- Heat oil in a stock pot. Add clams and stir for 2 minutes. Add lemon grass, ginger, chillies and onion and stir for 2 more minutes. Season with salt and pepper to taste.

- Add mirin and simmer mixture until liquid reduces to one quarter.

- Add chicken stock. Bring to the boil then reduce heat and simmer for 30 minutes. Remove clams as they open and set aside. Discard clams that remain closed. Strain liquid.

- Return strained liquid back to the pot. Bring to the boil. Add udon, clams and butter, if desired, and boil for 2 minutes.

- Stir in lemon juice. Ladle into serving bowls, garnish with sliced chillies and serve immediately.

When choosing live clams, choose clams that are closed and avoid those which are open, chipped or broken.

chilli prawn soba noodles

Unlike traditional Japanese food, chilli is added to this noodle dish to spice things up. Serve this as a filling appetiser or a light lunch.

Serves 2

Ingredients

Dried soba	250 g (9 oz)
Cooking oil	3 Tbsp
Red chilli	1, seeded and finely sliced into strips
Ginger	2.5-cm (1-in) knob, peeled and grated
Prawns (shrimps)	8, peeled with tails intact
Enokitake mushrooms	100 g (3$\frac{1}{2}$ oz), trimmed
Bean sprouts	85 g (3 oz)
Salt	$\frac{1}{2}$ tsp
Sugar	1 tsp
Miso soup	300 ml (10 fl oz / 1$\frac{1}{4}$ cups)
Spring onions (scallions)	3, cut into 2.5-cm (1-in) lengths

Method

- Bring a pot of salted water to the boil. Add soba and cook 2–3 minutes or until just tender. Drain, rinse under cold water and divide between 2 serving bowls.

- Heat oil in a wok. Add chilli and ginger and stir-fry for 30 seconds. Add prawns, stir-fry for 1 minute. Add mushrooms, bean sprouts, salt and sugar, and stir-fry for another 2–3 minutes. Remove from heat.

- Spoon mushroom and prawn mixture over noodles, then ladle in hot miso soup.

- Garnish with spring onions and serve immediately.

chilli coconut crab rice noodles

This rich noodle dish is elegant and tasty. Serve as an exotic appetiser or as a spicy side dish with other seafood dishes.

Serves 4

Ingredients

Rice sticks	250 g (8 oz)
Cooking oil	2 tsp
Red chillies	4, large, seeded and chopped
Ginger	2.5-cm (1-in) knob, peeled and finely chopped
Spring onions (scallions)	4, sliced
Coconut milk	150 ml (5 fl oz / $^2/_3$ cup)
Thai fish sauce	1 Tbsp
Crabmeat	250 g (9 oz)

Method

• Soak rice sticks in boiling water for 15–20 minutes or until soft. Drain well and set aside.

• Heat oil in a wok over high heat. Add chillies, ginger and spring onions and cook for 2 minutes.

• Add rice sticks, coconut milk, fish sauce and crabmeat. Toss to combine and remove from heat.

• Divide rice sticks among 4 individual serving bowls and serve hot.

mee siam
(rice vermicelli in spicy gravy)

Mee Siam a fabulous luncheon dish that is made from a Malay-style gravy. The gravy is given an intriguing flavour by the addition of salted soy beans, and the finished dish is liberally sprinkled with lime or lemon juice for further titillation of the taste buds and nose!

Serves 4–6

Ingredients

Cooking oil for deep-frying	
Firm bean curd	2, each 200 g (7 oz), cut into small cubes
Bean sprouts	500 g (1 lb 1½ oz)
Cooked prawns	375 g (12 oz), peeled
Chives (*kucai*) or spring onions (scallions)	85 g (3 oz), cut into 2.5-cm (1-in) lengths
Rice vermicelli	500 g (1 lb 1½ oz), soaked to soften and drained
Eggs	3, hardboiled, peeled and halved
Limes or lemons	2, halved

Spice Paste

Dried red chillies	10, soaked and drained
Shallots	12
Lemon grass	1 stalk
Dried prawn (shrimp) paste (*belacan*)	1 tsp
Cooking oil	3 Tbsp
Salted soy beans (*taucheo*)	2 Tbsp, lightly crushed
Salt	1 tsp
Sugar	1 Tbsp

Gravy

Coconut milk	1.25 litres (40 fl oz / 5 cups)
Tamarind concentrate	60 ml (2 fl oz / ¼ cup)
Warm water	125 ml (4 fl oz / ½ cup)

Method

- Prepare spice paste. Combine chillies, shallots, lemon grass and dried prawn paste in a blender (processor) until a paste is formed.

- Heat oil in a wok. Fry spice paste for 3–4 minutes. Add salted soy beans and cook for 1 minute, stirring constantly.

- Sprinkle in salt and sugar and continue frying for another minute. Remove half this mixture to prepare gravy. Set aside wok with remaining mixture.

- Prepare gravy. Put half the fried spice paste into a large saucepan and add coconut milk. Bring to the boil, stirring constantly, then add tamarind. Simmer for 2–3 minutes, stirring constantly, then set aside.

- Heat oil for deep-frying. Deep-fry bean curd until golden brown. Drain well and set aside.

- Just before serving, heat remaining spice mixture left in the wok, then add bean sprouts and cook over high heat, stirring constantly, for 1 minute.

- Add half the cooked prawns and half the chopped chives. Cook for about 30 seconds, stirring constantly.

- Add rice vermicelli a little at a time, stirring vigorously to mix well with other ingredients. Repeat until vermicelli is used up.

- Transfer to a serving dish. Arrange remaining prawns, chives or spring onions, eggs and fried bean curd on top. Ladle gravy over and serve with lime or lemon halves.

squid ink fettucine

This squid lover's delight is a lovely combination of squid rings, squid ink pasta and a spicy tomato sauce. Serve with a chilled glass of white wine.

Serves 2

Ingredients

Squid ink fettucine	200 g (7 oz)
Olive oil	3 Tbsp
Garlic	1 clove, peeled and chopped
Shallot	1, peeled and sliced
Crushed chilli flakes	1/2 tsp
Squid rings	150 g (5 oz)
Salt	to taste
Ground black pepper	to taste
Canned chopped tomatoes	200 g (7 oz)

Method

- Bring a pot of salted water to the boil. Add pasta and cook until al dente. Drain and set aside in a large bowl.

- Heat oil in a medium frying pan. Add garlic, shallot and chilli flakes and fry for 2 minutes.

- Season squid with salt and pepper then add to frying pan and fry for another minute.

- Add tomatoes and fry for 2–3 minutes or until tomatoes are heated through. Remove from heat.

- Pour over pasta and mix well. Transfer to serving dish and serve immediately.

fried glass noodles

This recipe allows the bland glass noodles to absorb flavours from the delectable stock. Serve this as a meal on its own or as part as a Chinese meal.

Serves 2

Ingredients

Dark soy sauce	1 tsp
Light soy sauce	1 tsp
Sesame oil	1 tsp
Salt	1 tsp
Ground white pepper	1/2 tsp
Chicken stock	500 ml (16 fl oz / 2 cups)
Glass (transparent) noodles	120 g (4 oz)
Chicken drumstick	1, deboned and cut into strips
Prawns (shrimps)	120 g (4 oz), medium, peeled with tails intact
Dried Chinese mushrooms	4, soaked to soften and cut into strips
Cooking oil	4 Tbsp
Shallots	3, peeled and diced
Garlic	2 cloves, peeled and sliced
Ginger	2.5-cm (1-in), peeled and cut into strips
Red chillies	2, cut into strips
Spring onions (scallions)	2, cut into 2.5-cm (1-in) lengths
Sambal belacan (optional)	

Seasoning

Salt	1/2 tsp
Ground white pepper	1/4 tsp
Light soy sauce	1 tsp
Corn flour (cornstarch)	1 tsp

Mushroom Seasoning

Light soy sauce	1/2 tsp
Sesame oil	1/4 tsp
Sugar	1/4 tsp

Method

- Combine light and dark soy sauce, sesame oil, salt, pepper and chicken stock in a large saucepan. Soak noodles in stock for at least 30 minutes or until soft.

- Season chicken and prawns with seasoning and set aside.

- Season mushrooms with mushroom seasoning and set aside.

- Heat oil in wok. Add shallots, garlic and ginger and fry until shallots are lightly browned. Add mushrooms and stir-fry for 1 minute.

- Add chicken and prawns and stir-fry for 2 minutes. Pour in stock and noodle mixture and stir-fry until liquid evaporates and mixture is almost dry.

- Sprinkle in chillies and spring onions and mix well. Serve hot with *sambal belacan*, if desired.

poultry

chinese-style fried noodles

Chow Mein is one of the best known Chinese dishes. This quick-to-prepare and delicious dish is ideal for a mid-week meal.

Serves 4

Ingredients

Thin yellow egg noodles or spaghetti	450 g (1 lb)
French beans	220 g (8 oz), trimmed and sliced
Cooking oil	60 ml (2 fl oz / ¼ cup)
Shallots	2, peeled and thinly sliced
Garlic	1 clove, peeled and crushed
Cooked chicken breast	110 g (4 oz), finely shredded
Dried Chinese mushrooms	3, soaked to soften, stems discarded and sliced
Light soy sauce	2 Tbsp
Sugar	1 tsp
Chinese cooking wine (*hua tiao*)	1 Tbsp
Butter	1½ Tbsp
Chicken stock	3 Tbsp
Chicken stock cube	½ , crumbled

Method

- Bring a pot of salted water to the boil. Add noodles or spaghetti and cook until just tender. Drain well, set aside and keep warm.

- Half fill a medium saucepan with salted water and bring it to the boil. Add beans and boil for 5 minutes. Drain and set aside.

- In a large frying pan, heat oil over moderate heat. Add shallots and garlic and fry, stirring constantly, for 2 minutes.

- Add chicken and mushrooms and stir-fry for 1 minute. Add soy sauce, sugar and wine and continue to stir-fry for 1½ minutes. Set aside with beans and keep warm.

- Using the same pan, add butter, chicken stock and stock cube. When butter has melted, add noodles. Cook, stirring and turning constantly, for 2 minutes or until noodles or spaghetti are heated through. Transfer to a serving dish.

- Return beans, mushrooms and chicken mixture to the frying pan and heat through.

- Spoon mixture over noodles. Mix well and serve immediately.

chicken tarragon pasta

Quick and easy to put together, this pasta dish consists of crispy chicken fillets and a light tarragon flavoured cream sauce.

Serves 3

Ingredients

Spinach fettucine	255 g (9 oz)
Cooking oil for deep-frying	
Chicken breast fillets	2, cut into small pieces
Corn flour (cornstarch)	100 g (3$\frac{1}{2}$ oz)
Olive oil	2 Tbsp
Garlic	2 cloves, peeled and chopped
Light (single) cream	150 ml (5 fl oz / $\frac{5}{8}$ cup)
Chopped tarragon leaves	3 Tbsp
Spinach leaves	100 g (4 oz) , thick stems removed
Salt	to taste
Ground black pepper	to taste
Lemon	1, sliced into wedges

Method

- Bring a pot of salted water to the boil. Add fettucine and cook until al dente.

- Meanwhile, heat oil for deep-frying. Just before frying, coat chicken evenly with corn flour. Deep-fry until golden brown and drain well.

- Heat olive oil in a large frying pan. Add garlic, then stir in cream, tarragon and 3 Tbsp water from pasta pot. Heat through over low heat.

- When pasta is cooked, add spinach into the same pot and cook for 1 minute. Drain spinach and pasta mixture.

- Add pasta and spinach to sauce and toss well. Season with salt and pepper. Transfer to a serving dish. Serve immediately with chicken and lemon wedges.

green chicken curry noodles

This easy version of Green Chicken Curry Noodles uses the convenience of store bought green curry paste, reducing the hassle of preparing it from scratch.

Serves 4

Ingredients

Coconut cream	125 ml (4 fl oz / $\frac{1}{2}$ cup)
Green curry paste	2 Tbsp
Chicken thighs fillet	4, cut into 2.5-cm (1-in) pieces
Coconut milk	375 ml (12 fl oz / $1\frac{1}{2}$ cups)
Kaffir lime leaves	4, torn
Thai fish sauce	1 Tbsp
Chopped palm sugar	2 tsp
Fresh coriander leaves (cilantro)	55 g (2 oz)
Chopped fresh basil leaves	55 g (2 oz)
Salt	a pinch
Rice sticks	250 g (9 oz), soaked in hot water to soften and drained
Red chilli	1, seeded and cut into strips

Method

- Place coconut cream in a wok. Heat over medium heat for 5 minutes until a film of oil appears on the surface.

- Add curry paste and cook, stirring for 2 minutes or until fragrant.

- Add chicken, coconut milk, lime leaves and fish sauce, and bring to the boil over high heat. Reduce heat to medium and simmer, stirring occasionally, for 10 minutes or until chicken is cooked through.

- Add palm sugar and cook, stirring constantly, for 1 minute or until sugar dissolves. Remove from heat. Stir in coriander and basil. Season with salt.

- Divide noodles into 4 bowls and spoon curry over noodles. Garnish with chilli and serve immediately.

spicy chicken soup with noodles

Known to the Indonesians as Mee Soto, *this noodle soup is popular because of its spicy broth that is earthy and heady. Serve with sambal if you enjoy extra spiciness.*

Serves 4

Ingredients

Chicken pieces	450 g (1 lb)
Water	1 litre (32 fl oz / 4 cups)
Salt	1 tsp
Kaffir lime leaf	1
Thick rice vermicelli	200 g (7 oz)
Potato	1, boiled, peeled and diced
Bean sprouts	100 g (3½ oz) scalded
Spinach or silver beet leaves	a handful, blanched
Eggs	2, hardboiled, peeled and halved

Spice Mix

Black peppercorns	1 tsp
Coriander leaves (cilantro)	1 tsp
Candlenuts	4
Garlic	1–2 cloves, peeled
Shallots	4–6, peeled
Ginger	1-cm (½-in) knob, peeled
Ground turmeric	¼ tsp
Cooking oil	2 Tbsp

Garnish (optional)

Fried shallots
Fresh coriander
  leaves

Method

- Simmer chicken in water and salt until tender. Remove from heat and set aside to cool in liquid. Strain, remove and shred chicken. Reserve stock.

- Prepare spice mix. Combine all ingredients except oil in a blender (processor) until a fine paste is formed.

- Heat in a heavy saucepan and gently fry spice mixture for 3–5 minutes. Add reserved stock and lime leaf, cover pan, and simmer for 10 minutes.

- Divide vermicelli, potato, bean sprouts, vegetables, eggs and chicken among 4 serving bowls. Ladle in soup, garnish as desired and serve immediately.

For a richer variation, add
125 ml (4 fl oz / ½ cup) coconut
milk when frying spice mixture.

udon with chicken and spring onions

Udon dishes are a popular lunch meal in Japan. This filling bowl of udon soup consists of chicken, shiitake mushrooms, cabbage and a garnishing of spring onions.

Serves 4–6

Ingredients

Dashi	2 litres (64 fl oz / 8 cups)
Salt	2 tsp
Dark soy sauce	3 Tbsp
Light soy sauce	3 Tbsp
Sugar	2 Tbsp
Mirin	2 Tbsp
Chicken breasts	450 g (1 lb), cut into bite-sized pieces
Spring onions (scallions)	6, halved lengthways then cut 5-cm (2-in) lengths
Shiitake mushrooms	6–8, wiped clean and stems discarded
Cabbage	¼ head, cut into squares
Udon	450 g (1 lb)

Method

- In a large pot, bring dashi to the boil. Add salt, soy sauces, sugar and mirin. Stir until sugar dissolves.

- Bring broth back to the boil and add chicken. Simmer for 10 minutes or until chicken is tender. Skim off any foam that rises to the surface.

- Add spring onions, mushrooms and cabbage and simmer for another 2–3 minutes.

- Meanwhile, bring a large pot of water to the boil. Add udon, stir and cook for 3 minutes or until udon is tender. Drain and rinse under cold running water then drain again.

- Divide noodles equally among 4–6 serving bowls. Ladle hot dashi broth over udon and serve immediately.

Ready-made dashi is available at most Asian supermarkets.

poached soy chicken with crispy noodles

The crispy noodle stack provides a crispy texture and is visually stunning when served to guests. Serve as a filling appetiser or a light meal.

Serves 4

Ingredients

Snow peas	100 g (3½ oz), trimmed
Rice sticks	125 g (4 oz)
Light soy sauce	125 ml (4 fl oz / ½ cup) + 1 Tbsp
Cooking oil for deep-frying	
Chicken stock	125 ml (4 fl oz / ½ cup)
Chicken breast fillets	4

Method

- Bring a pot of salted water to the boil. Blanch snow peas for 3 minutes. Drain, set aside and keep warm.

- Soak rice sticks in boiling water for 10–15 minutes or until soft. Drain well and transfer to a bowl. Toss with 1 Tbsp soy sauce and divide into 12 equal portions.

- Heat oil for deep-frying. Add 2–3 portions of noodles and deep-fry for 30 seconds to 1 minute or until golden and crisp. Drain well. Repeat with remaining noodles.

- Combine remaining soy sauce and chicken stock in a frying pan and bring to a simmer. Add chicken and cook for 4 minutes on each side or until cooked through. Remove from heat, slice chicken and reserve liquid.

- To serve, place one piece of deep-fried noodle on a serving plate followed by a layer of chicken. Repeat layering and end with a piece of deep-fried noodles.

- Arrange snow peas around chicken and noodles. Drizzle with reserved liquid and serve immediately.

egg noodles chiang mai

Egg Noodles Chiang Mai can be prepared the day before, but only add herbs just before serving or they will lose their freshness. Serve as a light lunch or as part of a Thai meal.

Serves 4

Ingredients

Dried egg noodles	200 g (7 oz)
Cooked chicken breast	350 g (12 oz), shredded
Red onion	1/2, peeled and sliced thinly
Fresh coriander leaves (cilantro)	6 sprigs
Fresh mint leaves	3 sprigs
Cooking oil	3 Tbsp
Lime	1, grated for zest and squeezed for juice
Thai fish sauce	1 tsp
Ginger	1-cm (1/2-in) knob, peeled and grated
Garlic	1 clove, peeled and crushed
Red chilli	1, seeded and chopped

Method

- Bring a pot of water to the boil. Add noodles and cook for 5 minutes or until tender. Drain, rinse under cold water and drain again. Transfer to a serving dish.

- Add chicken, onion, coriander and mint to noodles.

- Combine oil, lime zest and juice, fish sauce, ginger, garlic and chilli in a bowl. Pour over noodles and mix well. Refrigerate for 1 hour or until ready to serve.

chicken soup noodles

This all-time favourite noodle soup traditionally consists of a clear chicken broth and pieces of chicken and vegetables. This comforting version of Chicken Noodle Soup uses cabbage, carrot, mushrooms and chicken.

Serves 6

Ingredients

Cooking oil	1 Tbsp
Onion	1, peeled and minced
Garlic	2 cloves, peeled and minced
Minced ginger	2 tsp
Carrot	1, sliced
Cabbage	½ head, small, sliced
Chicken stock	1.5 litres (48 fl oz / 6 cups)
Dried Chinese mushrooms	30 g (1 oz), soaked to soften, stems discarded and sliced
Salt	to taste
Cooked chicken breast	3, shredded
Dried egg noodles or ramen	300 g (10½ oz)
Spring onions (scallions)	2, chopped

Seasoning

Light soy sauce	1 Tbsp
Rice vinegar	2 Tbsp
Sesame oil	to taste

Method

- Heat oil in a large saucepan over moderate heat. Add onion, garlic and ginger, and cook, stirring occasionally, for 3 minutes. Add carrot and cabbage and toss to combine.

- Add stock, mushrooms and salt to taste and simmer for 10 minutes. Add chicken and seasoning. Simmer, stirring occasionally for 3 minutes or until chicken breast is heated through.

- Bring a pot of salted water to the boil. Add noodles and boil for 3 minutes or until tender. Drain and divide noodles among 6 serving bowls.

- Ladle soup into bowls, garnish with spring onions and serve immediately.

pesto chicken pasta

Pesto is an Italian sauce that differs from region to region in Italy. This pesto is a classic version using garlic, pine nuts, basil, olive oil and Parmesan cheese. When buying Parmesan cheese, look out for Parmigiano-Reggiano as it has the best flavour.

Serves 4

Ingredients

Angel hair	400 g (1 lb 2 oz)
Cooked chicken	350 g (12 oz), cut into chunks
Lemon	1, squeezed for juice
Olive oil	3 Tbsp
Salt	to taste
Ground black pepper	to taste

Pesto

Garlic	2 cloves, roughly chopped
Pine nuts	55 g (2 oz)
Fresh basil leaves	1 cup
Olive oil	60 ml (2 fl oz / 1/4 cup)
Grated Parmesan cheese	55 g (2 oz)

Method

- Prepare pesto. Combine pesto ingredients in a mortar and pestle or a blender (processor) until a fine paste is formed. Set aside.

- Bring a pot of salted water to the boil. Add angel hair and cook until al dente. Drain well and transfer to a large bowl.

- Add chicken and 2 Tbsp pesto or more, if desired, lemon juice and olive oil to pasta, toss and mix well. Season with salt and pepper to taste.

- Transfer to a serving dish, top with 1/2 tsp pesto and serve immediately.

To make a vegan pesto, omit Parmesan cheese from recipe.

stir-fried duck noodles

This roasted duck noodle dish is a home-made version of the popular Cantonese roasted duck noodles. Serve as a meal on its own or as part of a Chinese banquet.

Serves 4

Ingredients

Cooking oil	2 Tbsp
Ginger	1 slice
Garlic	1 clove, peeled and crushed
Celery	2 stalks, finely chopped
Red chilli	1, finely chopped
Spring onions (scallions)	3, chopped
Roast duck	1/2, meat shredded
Yellow egg noodles	400 g (14 oz)
Bean sprouts	200 g (7 oz) , tailed

Seasoning

Chinese cooking wine (*hua tiao*)	1 Tbsp
Hoisin sauce	1 Tbsp
Oyster sauce	2 Tbsp
Light soy sauce	2 Tbsp
Sugar	to taste

Method

- Heat oil in a wok. Add ginger and garlic and cook until golden. Strain and reserve flavoured oil.

- Return oil to wok. Add celery, chilli and half the spring onions and stir-fry for 2 minutes. Add duck meat and stir-fry another 1 minute.

- Bring a pot of water to the boil. Add noodles and boil for 1 minute. Drain well and add to the wok. Toss ingredients and mix well.

- Add bean sprouts and toss. Add seasoning, toss and mix well. Transfer to a serving dish, garnish with remaining spring onions and serve.

hoisin duck noodles

This recipe is quick and simple to prepare because it uses store bought roasted duck.

Serves 2

Ingredients

Rice sticks	200 g (7 oz), soaked in hot water to soften and drained
Cucumber	1, cut into long thin sticks
Spring onions (scallions)	5, cut into 5-cm (2-in) lengths
Roasted duck	300 g (10½ oz), sliced

Sauce

Hoisin sauce	200 ml (7 fl oz / ⅘ cup)
Rice vinegar	60 ml (2 fl oz / ¼ cup)
Red chilli	1, small, seeded and finely chopped

Method

- Prepare sauce. Combine Hoisin sauce, rice vinegar and chilli in a small bowl. Mix well and set aside.

- Place rice sticks and cucumber in a bowl. Pour half the sauce over. Toss and mix well.

- Transfer rice sticks to a serving dish and garnish as desired. Serve noodles with duck and remaining sauce on the side.

meat

tan mein
(soup noodles)

Tan Mein is a popular noodle dish that eaten all over China as a meal or snack.

Serves 4–6

Ingredients

Thin yellow egg noodles or spaghetti	350 g (12 oz)
Cooking oil	1¹⁄₂ Tbsp
Onion	1, small, peeled and thinly sliced
Ginger	1.25-cm (¹⁄₂-in) knob, peeled and minced
Lean pork	220 g (8 oz), finely shredded
Butter	1 Tbsp
Shiitake mushrooms	100 g (4 oz), caps wiped and sliced
Cabbage	100 g (4 oz), sliced, blanched for 5 minutes and drained
Bean sprouts	100 g (4 oz), blanched for 1 minute and drained
Light soy sauce	1¹⁄₂ Tbsp
Sugar	1 tsp
Water	300 ml (10 fl oz / 1¹⁄₄ cups)
Chicken stock cube	1, crumbled
Chicken stock	625 ml (20 fl oz / 2¹⁄₂ cups)

Method

- Bring a pot of salted water to the boil. Add noodles and cook for 5–6 minutes or cook spaghetti for 10 minutes. Drain, set aside and keep warm.

- Heat oil in a large frying pan over moderate heat. Add onion, ginger and pork and fry, stirring constantly for 2 minutes.

- Add butter. When butter melts, add mushrooms, cabbage and bean sprouts. Stir-fry for 2 minutes.

- Stir in soy sauce and sugar and continue to stir-fry for another 1 minute. Remove pan from heat. Set aside and keep warm.

- In a large saucepan, bring water to the boil. Reduce heat to moderate, add stock cube and stir to dissolve.

- Add pork mixture and stock and bring mixture to the boil. Stir in noodles and simmer for 3 minutes.

- Divide noodles and soup among 4–6 serving bowls and serve immediately.

spaghetti with bacon in tomato sauce

A sumptuous Roman recipe, Spaghetti all' Amatriciana may be served with a mixed salad, crusty bread and a chilled white wine.

Serves 4-6

Ingredients

Olive oil	2 Tbsp
Onion	1, large, peeled and thinly sliced
Garlic	2 cloves, peeled and crushed
Bacon	6 slices, diced
Dry white wine	60 ml (2 fl oz / 1/4 cup)
Canned peeled tomatoes	450 g (1 lb), drained
Salt	1/2 tsp
Ground black pepper	1 tsp
Dried oregano	1/2 tsp
Cooked spaghetti	450 g (1 lb), drained and kept hot

Method

- Heat oil in a medium saucepan over moderate heat. Add onion and garlic. Fry, stirring occasionally, for 5–7 minutes or until onion is soft and translucent but not brown.

- Stir in bacon and cook for a further 4 minutes, stirring constantly.

- Add wine and bring liquid to the boil for 2 minutes, then add tomatoes, salt, pepper and oregano. Reduce heat to low and continue cooking for a further 15 minutes, stirring occasionally. Remove pan from heat.

- Place spaghetti in a large, deep serving dish and ladle over sauce. Toss pasta until thoroughly coated.

- Transfer to a serving dish, garnish as desired and serve immediately.

shichimi-spiced beef ramen

This bowl of ramen is a delicious combination of hot beef stock and piquant beef.

Serves 2

Ingredients

Sirloin steak	200 g (7 oz), sliced
Cooking oil	1 tsp
Japanese seven-spice seasoning (*shichimi*)	2 tsp
Salt	½ tsp
Ramen noodles	250 g (9 oz)
Beef stock	1 litre (32 fl oz / 4 cups)
Chinese flowering cabbage (*choy sum*)	110 g (4 oz)
Spring onions (scallions)	4, finely sliced

Method

- Rub sirloin with oil. Season with spice powder and salt then set aside to marinate for 5 minutes.

- Heat a frying pan over medium heat until almost smoking. Cook beef for 4 minutes on each side or until cooked. Set aside and keep warm.

- Bring a large saucepan of salted water to the boil. Add noodles and cook for 2–3 minutes or until just tender. Drain and divide between 2 serving bowls.

- Bring stock to the boil. Add Chinese flowering cabbage and cook for 1 minute then ladle over noodles.

- Thinly slice beef at a slight angle and place on top of noodles. Garnish with spring onions and serve.

spaghetti with meatballs and tomato sauce

This recipe is delicious and incredibly easy to eat. Serve as a main course with a tossed green salad and garlic bread.

Serves 4

Ingredients

Cooked spaghetti	450 g (1 lb), drained and kept hot
Butter	30 g (1 oz)
Grated Parmesan cheese	100 g (4 oz)

Meatballs

White bread	2 thick slices, crusts removed
Milk	60 ml (2 fl oz / $\frac{1}{4}$ cup)
Minced beef	900 g (2 lb)
Dry white breadcrumbs	30 g (1 oz)
Grated Parmesan cheese	30 g (1 oz)
Egg	1, lightly beaten
Salt	$\frac{1}{2}$ tsp
Ground black pepper	$\frac{1}{2}$ tsp
Dried thyme	1 tsp
Grated lemon zest	2 tsp
Garlic	1 clove, peeled and crushed
Butter	100 g (4 oz)

Tomato Sauce

Butter	50 g (2 oz)
Onion	1, large, peeled and finely chopped
Garlic	2 cloves, peeled and crushed
Canned tomatoes	700 g (1$\frac{1}{2}$ lb)
Tomato purée	70 g (2$\frac{1}{2}$ oz)
Salt	$\frac{1}{2}$ tsp
Ground black pepper	$\frac{1}{2}$ tsp
Dried oregano	$\frac{1}{2}$ tsp

Method

- Prepare meatballs. In a small bowl, soak bread in milk for 5 minutes, or until milk is completely absorbed. Transfer soaked bread to a large mixing bowl.

- Add remaining meatball ingredients except butter to the bowl. Using your hands, mix and knead ingredients until well combined. Divide into 30 equal portions and roll into balls. Transfer onto a baking tray and chill in the refrigerator for 30 minutes.

- Meanwhile, prepare tomato sauce. In a large saucepan, melt butter over moderate heat. When foam subsides, add onion and garlic and cook, stirring occasionally for 5–7 minutes or until onion is soft and translucent but not brown.

- Stir in tomatoes with juice from can, tomato purée, salt, pepper and oregano. Bring liquid to the boil, stirring occasionally. Reduce heat to low, cover pan and simmer sauce for 35 minutes.

- Remove meatballs from refrigerator. Melt butter in a large frying pan over moderate heat. When foam subsides, add meatballs, a few at a time, and cook, turning occasionally, for 6–8 minutes or until evenly browned. Drain well and set aside.

- Add meatballs into tomato sauce and cover pan. Continue to simmer for a further 20–30 minutes or until meatballs are cooked. Remove from heat.

- Place spaghetti in a large, deep serving dish and add butter. Toss spaghetti until butter has melted.

- Spoon sauce and meatballs over spaghetti. Sprinkle Parmesan cheese over and serve immediately.

yang chow noodles

Yang Chow Noodles is a variation of a Chinese recipe consisting of thinly sliced pork, spring onions and celery in a slightly sweet sour sauce served on a bed of succulent noodles.

Serves 3

Ingredients

Cooking oil	3 Tbsp
Lean pork	450 g (1 lb), thinly sliced
Shallots	2, peeled and chopped
Celery	2 stalks, trimmed and thinly sliced
Chicken stock	125 ml (4 fl oz / 1/2 cup)
Light soy sauce	1 Tbsp
Cayenne pepper	1/2 tsp
White button mushrooms	110 g (4 oz), caps wiped and thinly sliced
Soft brown sugar	1 Tbsp
Corn flour (cornstarch)	2 Tbsp, mixed with 1 Tbsp water
Thick yellow egg noodles	220 g (8 oz)

Method

- Heat 2 Tbsp oil in a frying pan over high heat.

- Add pork and fry, stirring constantly, for 8 minutes or until lightly and evenly browned. Reduce heat to moderate and add shallots and celery. Fry, stirring occasionally for a further 5 minutes.

- Stir in chicken stock, soy sauce, cayenne pepper, mushrooms, sugar and corn flour mixture.

- Bring liquid to the boil, stirring constantly, and cook for 10 minutes or until sauce has thickened. Cover pan tightly and remove from heat. Keep hot.

- Bring a pot of water to the boil. Add noodles and cook for 6–8 minutes until just tender. Drain well and transfer to a large mixing bowl and toss with remaining oil.

- Transfer noodles to a serving dish and spoon pork mixture over. Serve immediately.

hot sour noodles

As its name suggests, the broth of this noodle dish is hot and sour. Serve as part of a Chinese meal.

Serves 2

Ingredients

Minced pork	125 g (4½ oz)
Cooking oil	2½ Tbsp
Dried egg noodles	300 g (10½ oz)
Dried prawns (shrimps)	30 g (1 oz), washed and chopped
Sichuan preserved vegetable (*char choy*)	125 g (4½ oz) washed and diced
Peanuts	30 g (1 oz), roasted and chopped
Roasted white sesame seeds	30 g (1 oz)
Spring onion (scallion)	1, chopped

Pork Seasoning

Ground white pepper	½ tsp
Salt	¼ tsp
Light soy sauce	½ tsp

Soup

Chicken stock	1.5 litres (48 fl oz / 6 cups)
Sugar	2 tsp
Salt	½ tsp
Dark soy sauce	1 Tbsp
Light soy sauce	3 Tbsp
Black vinegar	1 Tbsp
Chilli sauce	2 Tbsp
Sesame oil	1 Tbsp
Chilli oil	1 Tbsp

Method

- Season minced pork with seasoning and set aside.

- Bring a saucepan of water to a boil and add ½ Tbsp oil. Add noodles and cook for 5 minutes or until just tender. Strain and divide equally between individual serving bowls.

- Heat remaining oil in a large saucepan and fry dried prawns until fragrant.

- Add Sichuan preserved vegetable and minced pork. Stir fry for 1 minute.

- Add soup ingredients and bring to the boil. Ladle soup into serving bowls over noodles. Sprinkle with chopped peanuts, sesame seeds and spring onion. Serve hot.

beefy spaghetti bake

Serve this dish with crusty French bread and butter, and a green salad tossed in French dressing.

Serves 4

Ingredients

Butter	75 g (3 oz)
Onions	2, peeled and chopped
Minced beef	350 g (12 oz)
Canned tomatoes	225 g (8 oz)
Dried mixed herbs	1 tsp
Salt	to taste
Ground black pepper	to taste
Spaghetti	100 g (4 oz) , broken into short lengths
Grated Parmesan cheese	2 Tbsp
Dried breadcrumbs	25 g (1 oz)
Grated Cheddar cheese	50 g (2 oz)

Sauce

Egg	1, beaten
Plain (all-purpose) flour	25 g (1 oz)
Milk	300 ml (10 fl oz / ¾ cup)
Grated Cheddar cheese	50 g (2 oz)

Method

- Heat oven to 190°C (375°F).

- Melt 25 g (1 oz) butter in a frying pan. Add onions and fry until soft. Add minced beef and fry over moderate heat until well browned, stirring constantly to break up lumps.

- Stir in tomatoes, herbs, salt and pepper to taste and continue cooking for a further 10–15 minutes. Set aside.

- Meanwhile, bring a pan of salted water to the boil. Add spaghetti and cook pasta until al dente. Drain well.

- Using the same pan, melt 25 g (1 oz) butter, add Parmesan cheese and spaghetti. Toss well to mix over gentle heat.

- Place half the spaghetti in the bottom of a buttered ovenproof dish. Spread meat mixture evenly over, then top with remaining spaghetti.

- Prepare sauce. Whisk egg and flour together in a small saucepan then gradually stir in milk and Cheddar cheese.

- Place pan over gentle heat and heat through for about 5 minutes or until thickened, whisking constantly. Add salt and pepper to taste, then pour over spaghetti.

- Sprinkle breadcrumbs and Cheddar cheese over sauce, then dot with remaining butter. Bake in the oven for about 20 minutes until topping is golden brown. Remove from oven and serve hot.

crispy rice vermicelli with beef shreds

Crispy Rice Vermicelli with Beef Shreds make a tantalising dish to serve your guests. The crispy vermicelli provides a delightful crackle when eaten and an intriguing visual on the plate.

Serves 2

Ingredients

Beef	100 g (4 oz), thinly sliced
Carrot	1, peeled and shredded
Canned bamboo shoots	60 g (2 oz), shredded
Cooking oil for deep-frying	
Thin rice vermicelli	90 g (3 oz), broken into 5-cm (2-in) lengths
Ginger	2.5-cm (1-in), peeled and shredded
Garlic	1 clove, peeled and finely chopped
Dried Chinese mushrooms	2, soaked to soften, stems discarded and shredded
Green capsicum (bell pepper)	1/2, cut into thin strips

Marinade

Salt	1/4 tsp
Sugar	1/2 tsp
Corn flour (cornstarch)	1/2 tsp
Water	2 tsp
Cooking oil	1 Tbsp

Sauce

Salt	1/3 tsp
Sugar	1/3 tsp
Sesame oil	1/2 tsp
Oyster sauce	1 tsp
Chinese rice wine (*hua tiao*)	1/2 tsp
Dark soy sauce	1 tsp
Water	125 ml (4 fl oz / 1/2 cup)
Corn flour (cornstarch)	3/4 tsp

Method

- Season beef with marinade and set aside for at least 30 minutes.
- Bring a saucepan of salted water to the boil. Blanch carrot and bamboo shoots. Drain well and set aside.
- Heat oil for deep-frying. Add thin rice vermicelli and deep-fry until crispy. Drain well and transfer to a serving dish. Reserve 1 Tbsp oil.
- Heat a wok and add reserved oil. Lightly brown ginger and garlic. Add mushrooms and beef and stir-fry for 3 minutes.
- Add carrot, bamboo shoots and bean sprouts. Add capsicum and pour in sauce ingredients. When mixture bubbles and thickens, pour mixture over rice vermicelli and serve immediately.

dry pork chop noodles

Quick and easy to prepare, this picante Dry Pork Chop Noodles makes a delicious one-dish meal.

Serves 4

Ingredients

Cooking oil	3 Tbsp
Pork chops	350 g (12 oz)
Salt	to taste
Ground white pepper	to taste
Dried egg noodles	300 g (10½ oz)
Garlic	2 cloves, peeled and minced
Onions	2, peeled and sliced
Hot bean paste	1 Tbsp
Sichuan preserved vegetable (*char choy*)	90 g (3 oz), washed, cut into strips
Spring onions (scallions)	2, sliced

Sauce

Light soy sauce	½ Tbsp
Dark soy sauce	1 tsp
Chinese rice wine	1 Tbsp
Black vinegar	½ Tbsp
Chilli oil	1 Tbsp
Sesame oil	1 tsp
Ground white pepper	½ tsp
Sugar	2 tsp
Corn flour (cornstarch)	1 tsp
Pork stock	180 ml (6 fl oz / ¾ cup)

Method

- Heat 2 Tbsp oil in a frying pan over medium-high heat. Season pork chops with salt and pepper then fry pork chops for 3 minutes on each side or until golden brown. Drain, reserve oil and set aside.

- Bring a pot of salted water to the boil. Add noodles and cook for 3 minutes or until just tender. Drain and mix with reserved oil. Divide noodles equally among individual serving bowls.

- Prepare sauce. Combine all sauce ingredients in a bowl. Mix well and set aside.

- Heat remaining oil in a wok. Add garlic, onions and hot bean paste and stir-fry until fragrant.

- Add Sichuan preserved vegetable and stir-fry for 1 minute. Add sauce and simmer until thick. Remove from heat

- Add 2–3 Tbsp sauce into each serving dish and mix well. Garnish with spring onions and serve with pork chops.

lemon pork and noodle stir-fry

This Thai-style noodle dish gets its predominant lemony taste from lemon grass and kaffir lime leaves. Chicken can be substituted for pork if desired.

Serves 4

Ingredients

Pork fillet	450 g (1 lb), thinly sliced across the grain
Cooking oil	2 Tbsp
Lemon grass	1 stalk, finely chopped
Ginger	5-cm (2-in) knob, peeled and grated
Green chilli	1, seeded and finely chopped
Udon	400 g (14 oz)
Red onion	1, medium, peeled and cut into wedges
Sugar-snap peas	125 g (4½ oz), trimmed
Water	1 Tbsp
Kaffir lime leaves	3, torn
Mint leaves	55 g (2 oz)
Salt	to taste
Ground white pepper	to taste

Method

- Combine pork, 2 tsp oil, lemon grass, ginger and chilli in a bowl. Mix well and set aside.

- Bring a saucepan of salted water to the boil over high heat. Add udon and cook, stirring occasionally, for 4 minutes or until tender. Drain and keep warm.

- Heat 2 tsp oil in a wok over high heat until smoking. Add half the pork mixture and stir-fry for 2 minutes or until brown. Transfer to a bowl and keep warm. Repeat with remaining pork.

- Heat remaining oil in the same wok over medium heat until smoking. Add onion and stir-fry for 1 minute or until soft.

- Add sugar-snap peas and water, cover and cook for 1 minute or until peas are cooked.

- Return pork to wok. Add lime leaves and stir-fry for 2 minutes or until heated through. Remove from heat.

- Add mint and toss to combine. Season to taste with salt and pepper.

- Divide noodles among 4 individual serving bowls. Top with pork mixture, garnish as desired and serve immediately.

clear beef noodle soup

Clear Beef Noodle Soup, an everyday Vietnamese dish that is known as Pho Bo to the locals. Rump steak can be substituted with cooked brisket or flank steak and beef tripe and tendon can be added to the soup, if desired.

Serves 4

Ingredients

Beef stock	2 litres (64 fl oz / 8 cups)
Ginger	2.5-cm (1-in) knob, peeled and sliced
Bird's eye chillies	2, seeded and chopped
Lemon grass	1 stalk, cut into strips
Thai fish sauce	1 Tbsp
Lime juice	60 ml (2 fl oz / ¼ cup)
Rice sticks	375 g (13½ oz), soaked in hot water to soften and drained
Rump steak	500 g (1 lb 1½ oz), trimmed of fat, thinly sliced
Bean sprouts	100 g (3½ oz)
Spring onions (scallions)	2, chopped
Mint leaves	50 g (2 oz)
Lime	1, cut into wedges

Method

- Bring stock, ginger, chillies and lemon grass to the boil. Simmer for 10 minutes then strain. Add fish sauce and lime juice to taste and return soup to a simmer.

- Divide noodles among 4 serving bowls. Top with beef, bean sprouts, spring onions and mint.

- Pour boiling stock over and allow beef to poach briefly until cooked to your liking. Serve with lime wedges.

beef hor fun

For the best results, this Cantonese beef rice noodle dish requires a well-oiled hot wok to produce a concentrated flavour and aroma.

Serves 2

Ingredients

Beef	120 g (4½ oz), cut into thin slices
Bok choy	5 small stalks, ends trim
Cooking oil	2 Tbsp
Salt	½ tsp
Fresh flat rice noodles	300 g (10½ oz)
Light soy sauce	1 Tbsp, mixed with 1 Tbsp water
Bean sprouts	100 g, tailed

Marinade

Baking soda	⅓ tsp
Ginger juice	10 ml (⅓ fl oz)
Salt	½ tsp
Sugar	¼ tsp
Corn flour (cornstarch)	2 tsp
Cooking oil	1 Tbsp

Sauce

Beef stock	125 ml (4 fl oz / ½ cup)
Light soy sauce	½ tsp
Dark soy sauce	2 tsp
Corn flour (cornstarch)	1 Tbsp
Spring onion (scallion)	1, cut into 2.5-cm (1-in) lengths

Method

- Rub marinade ingredients into beef, adding oil last. Set aside for at least 20 minutes.

- Bring half a saucepan of salted water to the boil. Blanch bok choy for 3 minutes. Drain well, transfer to a serving dish and reserve water.

- Use reserved water to scald beef. Set aside for 1 minute then drain well and place on serving dish.

- Heat 1 Tbsp in a clean wok. Add rice noodles and toss for 2 minutes. Add combined sauce ingredients and stir-fry until well mixed. Remove and place on vegetables.

- Reheat wok with 1 Tbsp oil and stir-fry bean sprouts for 30 seconds. Spoon over fried noodles and serve immediately.

ramen soup with char siew and corn

Ramen noodles originated in China, but are now popular all over Japan. They are a wheat-based noodle that is traditionally served in a hot broth. In this version, ramen is served with a chicken broth, char siew, corn kernels and garnished with spring onions.

Serves 4

Ingredients

Ramen	200 g (7 oz)
Cooking oil	2 tsp
Ginger	1-cm (1/2-in) knob, peeled and grated
Chicken stock	1.5 litres (48 fl oz / 6 cups)
Mirin	2 Tbsp
Chinese roast pork (*char siew*)	200 g (7 oz), sliced
Corn kernels	125 g (41/2 oz)
Spring onions (scallions)	2, sliced + extra for garnishing
Unsalted butter (optional)	60 g (3 oz)

Method

- Bring a saucepan of salted water to the boil over high heat. Add ramen and cook for 4 minutes or until tender. Drain, rinse and divide among 4 individual serving bowls.

- Heat oil in a large saucepan over high heat. Stir-fry ginger for 1 minute. Add chicken stock and mirin and bring to the boil. Reduce heat and simmer for 8 minutes.

- Add roast pork and cook for 5 minutes, then add the corn kernels and spring onion and cook for another 3 minutes or until kernels are tender.

- Ladle soup over, then put 1 Tbsp butter, if desired on each serving. Garnish with extra spring onion and serve at once.

NOTE

The addition of 1 Tbsp butter at the end gives the soup a richer taste, but can be omitted for a healthier choice.

black bean mince stir-fry

Black bean sauce is made from fermented soy beans and spices. This strong flavoured sauce is a good complement to the bland tasting rice noodles. Using prepared black bean sauce makes the preparation of this dish a breeze.

Serves 4

Ingredients

Cooking oil	3 tsp
Garlic	2 cloves, peeled and finely chopped
Ginger	1-cm (1/2-in) knob, peeled and grated
Green capsicum (bell pepper)	1, white pith removed and sliced
Red chilli	1, sliced
Shiitake mushrooms	150 g (5 oz), caps wiped and sliced
Minced beef	450 g (1 lb)
Black bean sauce	2 Tbsp
Light soy sauce	2 Tbsp
Fresh flat rice noodles	400 g (14 oz), blanched

Method

- Heat oil in a wok over high heat. Stir-fry garlic and ginger for 30 seconds. Add capsicum and chilli, stir-fry for 1 minute. Add mushrooms and stir-fry for 1 minute, until tender. Transfer to a bowl.

- Reheat wok and stir-fry mince, breaking up any lumps. Cook for 5 minutes or until browned.

- Return capsicum and chilli to wok. Add black bean sauce and soy sauce and stir-fry for another 1 minute.

- Place noodles into a serving bowl and pour black bean mince mixture over. Serve immediately.

spaghetti bolognese

Spaghetti Bolognese originates from the city of Bologna in Italy. The sauce can be made in advance and frozen. When using frozen sauce, set aside in the refrigerator to thaw for 3–4 hours before use.

Serves 8

Ingredients

Olive oil	1 Tbsp
Bacon	6 slices, chopped
Onion	1, large, peeled and finely chopped
Celery	1 stalk, roughly chopped
Carrot	1, roughly chopped
Garlic	2–3 cloves, peeled and crushed
Minced beef	1 kg (2 lb 3 oz)
Canned diced tomatoes	400 g (14 oz)
Red wine	60 ml (2 fl oz / ¼ cup)
Tomato paste	2 Tbsp
Milk	60 ml (2 fl oz / ¼ cup)
Bay leaves	2
Spaghetti	400 g (14 oz)
Grated Parmesan cheese	

Method

- Heat oil in a large saucepan over high heat. Add bacon, onion, celery, carrot and garlic. Cook, stirring occasionally for 5 minutes, until vegetables have softened.

- Add mince. Cook for 5 minutes until well browned, breaking up any lumps with the back of a wooden spoon.

- Stir in tomatoes, wine, tomato paste, milk and bay leaves. Bring mixture to the boil then reduce heat and simmer for 15 minutes.

- Meanwhile, bring a large saucepan of salted water to the boil. Add spaghetti and cook until al dente. Drain and transfer to a serving dish.

- Pour meat sauce over spaghetti and toss well. Sprinkle Parmesan cheese over and serve immediately.

noodles in peking meat sauce

Also known as Cha Chieng Mein, *Noodles in Peking Meat Sauce is a peasant dish in China that is gradually becoming a classic. Serve as part of a Chinese meal or with dumplings. If egg noodles are unavailable, spaghetti can be used as a substitute.*

Serves 4

Ingredients

Dried egg noodles	450 g (1 lb)
Cooking oil	3 Tbsp
Onion	1, medium, peeled and sliced
Garlic	2 cloves, peeled and crushed
Ginger	1-cm ($^1/_2$-in), peeled and finely chopped
Minced lean pork	350 g (12 oz)
Sesame oil	1 Tbsp
Light soy sauce	75 ml ($2^1/_2$ fl oz / 5 Tbsp)
Chinese cooking wine (*hua tiao*)	2 Tbsp
Sugar	1 Tbsp
Corn flour (cornstarch)	1 Tbsp, dissolved in 60 ml (2 fl oz / $^1/_4$ cup) chicken stock
Spring onions (scallions)	2, chopped

Method

- Bring a saucepan of salted water to the boil over high heat. Add noodles and cook for 5 minutes or until just tender. Drain, set aside and keep warm.

- Heat oil in a large frying pan over moderate heat. Add onion, garlic and ginger and fry, stirring constantly for 2 minutes.

- Add pork and stir-fry for 5 minutes or until meat is browned.

- Stir in sesame oil, soy sauce, wine and sugar and stir-fry for 3 minutes.

- Add corn flour mixture and cook, stirring constantly, until meat sauce thickens and becomes glossy. Remove pan from heat.

- Divide noodles among 4 individual serving bowls. Ladle meat sauce over noodles, garnish with spring onions and serve immediately.

thai-style pork and chilli noodles

A delicious combination of minced pork, rice sticks, spring onions, bean sprouts and a lime-based sauce. This is also a tasty way to use up leftover minced pork or chicken.

Serves 4

Ingredients

Cooking oil	1 Tbsp
Minced pork	450 g (1 lb)
Garlic	2 cloves, peeled and crushed
Red chilli	1, chopped finely
Thai fish sauce	2 Tbsp
Sweet soy sauce	60 ml (2 fl oz / ¼ cup)
Lime juice	85 ml (2½ fl oz / ⅓ cup)
Rice sticks	200 g (7 oz), soaked to soften and drained
Spring onions (scallions)	4, sliced
Chopped coriander leaves (cilantro)	2 sprigs
Bean sprouts	240 g (8½ oz), tailed
Kaffir lime leaves	4, sliced

Method

- Heat oil in a wok. Stir-fry pork until browned. Add garlic and chilli and stir-fry until fragrant.

- Add fish sauce, sweet soy sauce and lime juice. Cook, stirring occasionally, until mixture comes to the boil and is slightly thickened.

- Add remaining ingredients. Toss and cook until heated through and noodles are well coated. Remove from heat.

- Transfer to a serving plate and serve immediately.

As a variation to this recipe, minced pork can also be replaced with the same amount of minced chicken.

mexican chilli spaghetti

A popular pasta dish in Mexico, Mexican Chilli Spaghetti makes an exciting and economical meal. If you like very spicy and hot foods, add another chilli to the sauce.

Serves 4

Ingredients

Olive oil	60 ml (2 fl oz / ¼ cup)
Bacon	4 slices, sliced
Onions	2, medium, peeled and thinly sliced
Garlic	1 clove, peeled and crushed
Spaghetti	220 g (8 oz), broken into 5-cm (2-in) lengths
Canned peeled tomatoes	400 g (14 oz), drained and chopped
Salt	½ tsp
Ground black pepper	¼ tsp
Dried oregano	1 tsp
Ground cumin	¼ tsp
Green chilli	1, sliced
Vegetable stock	625 ml (20 fl oz / 2½ cups)

Method

- In a large, deep-frying pan, heat oil over moderate heat. Add bacon, onions and garlic and cook, stirring occasionally for 5–7 minutes or until onions are soft and translucent but not brown.

- Stir in spaghetti, tomatoes, salt, pepper, oregano, cumin and chilli. Cook, stirring occasionally, for 5 minutes.

- Pour in vegetable stock and bring mixture to the boil over high heat. Reduce heat to low and simmer gently, stirring occasionally, for 10–15 minutes or until liquid has been absorbed.

- Transfer to 4 individual warmed serving dishes and serve immediately.

glossary

1. Black bean sauce

Chinese black bean sauce is made from fermented soy beans. The soy beans are dried, salted and fermented with garlic and spices then processed. This rich and salty sauce is commonly used in Asian stir-fries and noodles dishes. Prepared black bean sauce is available in Asian supermarkets.

2. Candlenuts

These hard, medium-sized, and beige-coloured nuts is also known as *buah keras* in Malay. These nuts are pounded into a paste and added to Southeast Asian curry pastes for its nutty flavour and is also used to thicken sauces. Candlenuts should not be eaten raw as its oil is toxic. Soak candlenuts for at least 30 minutes before using. Store candlenuts in an airtight container in the refrigerator or in the freezer.

3. Chinese black vinegar

Chinese black vinegar is made from rice, wheat, sorghum or millet. It has a complex and mildly sweet taste. This vinegar is sometimes referred to as *Chinkiang*, the name of the region where the best Chinese black vinegars come from. Use in stir-fries and Asian noodle dishes.

4. Chinese roast pork (*char siew*)

These pork strips have been seasoned with ingredients such as hoisin, sesame oil and soy sauce and dyed with red food colouring just before roasting over a charcoal grill. Slice to serve.

5. Chinese sausage (*lup cheong*)

These Chinese sausages are usually made with fatty pork and smoked with a variety of spices that vary from maker to maker. They are slim and firm and are similar to pepperoni and salami. These sweet and oily sausages are commonly added to Asian noodle and rice dishes for a rich flavour and aroma.

6. Chives (*kucai*)

Also known as Chinese or garlic chives, these chives have long grass-like flat leaves. They are stronger tasting than western chives and are commonly used in Chinese cooking.

7. Dried egg noodles

Dried egg noodles are made from wheat flour, egg and water. They come in a two forms of thickness—thin or medium. These versatile noodles can be added into soups, used in stir-fries or boiled and topped with sauce.

8. Dried prawns (shrimps)

These prawns have been steamed, salted and then sun-dried. Soak for at least 30 minutes and discard water before using. Dried shrimp can also be chopped, pounded or added whole to Thai salads and Asian rice dishes.

9. Dried prawn (shrimp) paste

Known also as *belacan*, dried prawn paste is made from small sun-dried prawns, which have been salted and pounded to a form a paste. This paste is often used as a base ingredient for sambal and other spicy Malay dishes.

10. Glass (transparent) noodles

Also known as cellophane or bean thread noodles, these thin noodles are made from mung bean flour. Soak noodles in water for 20 minutes or until soft before adding to stir-fries or soups. They are often used in Southeast Asian cooking.

11. Hoisin sauce

This reddish-brown sauce is thick, sticky and sweet. Hoisin is widely used in Chinese cooking and is also known as Peking sauce or Chinese barbecue sauce. Use to flavour meats, seafood or poultry. Store in refrigerator after opening.

12. Hot bean paste

Hot bean paste is reddish-brown and is also called chilli bean paste. This paste is made from pounding fermented soy beans and chillies. Use in small amounts as the chilli paste is very hot. Hot bean paste is available in bottles from Asian supermarkets. Store in refrigerator after opening.

13. Japanese seven-seasoning spice

Nanami or shichimi togarashi is a seasoning made mainly from sansho pepper, dried mandarin peel, nori shreds, poppu and sesame seeds. The ingredients used in the bottled blend varies slightly from maker to maker. Slightly spicy, this seasoning is often added to rice, noodles or soups for extra spice.

14. Kaffir lime leaves

These lime leaves are recognised by their two distinct sections and are also known as double lime leaves. These leaves are commonly used in Thai cooking and curries. Shred or tear the lime leaves before adding to soups, stir-fries or curries to release their aroma. These leaves are available frozen but are less aromatic than the fresh leaves.

15. Lemon grass

Also known as *serai* in Malay, this fragrant, herb is native to India. Lemon grass is widely used in Asian curries, stews, soups and salads. Remove the hard outer leaves then use only the bulbous end of the lemon grass. Bruise to extract more flavour.

16, 17, 18, 19, 20. Pasta

Pasta is the generic Italian name for a dough that is made from semolina flour, eggs, salt and water or milk. Unlike fresh pasta, dried pasta is only made with semolina flour and water. Pasta comes in a variety of forms, lengths and colours to suit the different types of sauces they are tossed with. Dried pasta is available in supermarkets and fresh or flavoured pastas can be bought at gourmet shops or Italian specialty shops.

Angel hair, also known as *Capelli d'Angelo*, is long, fine and delicate. This pasta is suitable for light and oil-based sauces.

Linguine is long, slim and flat. This pasta accomodates most sauces.

Spaghetti, the most popular pasta, is long and round. This pasta is suitable for thick, chunky, vegetable and seafood sauces.

Spinach fettucine is a greenish-brown colour and is made by adding puréed spinach into the basic pasta dough mixture.

Squid ink pasta. Squid ink pasta gets its black colour from squid ink which is added into the basic pasta dough mixture.

21. Ramen

The dried form of ramen is more commonly known as instant noodles. Instant noodles are cooked noodles, which have been preserved by the process of deep-frying. As its name instant noodles suggests, these wheat-based noodles can be cooked in a short time of about 3 minutes.

22, 23. Rice noodles

Rice noodles are made from rice flour and water and are available dried and fresh. The fresh noodles are available in different widths and shapes and are commonly used in Thai, Chinese, Malaysian, Vietnamese and Singaporean cooking.

Fresh flat rice noodle are also known as *kway teow* are rice noodle sheets that have been cut into 1-cm (¹/₂-in) wide ribbons. Wash noodles thoroughly or blanch before cooking. Store in an airtight container in the refrigerator and use within 2 days of purchase.

Dried rice noodles are also know as rice sticks. Rice sticks are classified according to their size—thin, medium and wide. Soak in hot water for 5–30 minutes, depending on thickness or until softened before use. Break noodles into shorter lengths if using for stir-fries. If fresh rice noodles are unavailable, substitute every 110 g (4 oz) fresh noodles with 30 g (1 oz) dried rice noodles.

24.   **25.**

27.

28.

24. Soba

Made from buckwheat flour, these nutritious Japanese noodle are rich in vitamin C, B1, B2, and E. Soba noodles are usually light brown in colour except for flavoured sobas such as *cha soba*, which is flavoured with tea. These noodles can be eaten cold with a dipping sauce or added to hot soups. Soba is available dried in health stores and Asian supermarkets.

25. Sun-dried tomatoes

Known also as *pomodori secchi* in Italian, sun-dried tomatoes have are red and have wrinkled skins. Sun-dried tomatoes are roma tomatoes that have been salted, seasoned with herbs and sun-dried. These tomatoes can be added into sauces, salads or sandwiches. Store in airtight containers.

26. Thick rice vermicelli

Also known as *laksa* noodles, thick rice vermicelli is made from rice flour. These noodles are thick, round, smooth and white in colour. Store fresh noodles in an airtight container in the refrigerator and use within 2–3 days of purchase.

27. Thick yellow egg noodles

Also known as Hokkien noodles, these thick, round, yellow-coloured noodles are made from wheat and egg. These fresh noodles should be thoroughly washed or blanched before cooked. Yellow egg noodles are sold pre-packed or fresh in Asian supermarkets.

28. Udon

This Japanese noodle is thick, firm and cream-coloured. Udon is made from wheat flour and is often served in a soy sauce-based broth in Japan. Udon is available fresh and dried. Store fresh udon in a container in the refrigerator and use within a few days of purchase.

Weights and Measures

Quantities for this book are given in Metric, Imperial and American (spoon and cup) measures. Standard spoon and cup measurements used are: 1 tsp = 5 ml, 1 Tbsp = 15 ml, 1 cup = 250 ml. All measures are level unless otherwise stated.

Liquid And Volume Measures

Metric	Imperial	American
5 ml	⅙ fl oz	1 teaspoon
10 ml	⅓ fl oz	1 dessertspoon
15 ml	½ fl oz	1 tablespoon
60 ml	2 fl oz	¼ cup (4 tablespoons)
85 ml	2½ fl oz	⅓ cup
90 ml	3 fl oz	⅜ cup (6 tablespoons)
125 ml	4 fl oz	½ cup
180 ml	6 fl oz	¾ cup
250 ml	8 fl oz	1 cup
300 ml	10 fl oz (½ pint)	1¼ cups
375 ml	12 fl oz	1½ cups
435 ml	14 fl oz	1¾ cups
500 ml	16 fl oz	2 cups
625 ml	20 fl oz (1 pint)	2½ cups
750 ml	24 fl oz (1⅕ pints)	3 cups
1 litre	32 fl oz (1⅗ pints)	4 cups
1.25 litres	40 fl oz (2 pints)	5 cups
1.5 litres	48 fl oz (2⅖ pints)	6 cups
2.5 litres	80 fl oz (4 pints)	10 cups

Oven Temperature

	°C	°F	Gas Regulo
Very slow	120	250	1
Slow	150	300	2
Moderately slow	160	325	3
Moderate	180	350	4
Moderately hot	190/200	375/400	5/6
Hot	210/220	410/425	6/7
Very hot	230	450	8
Super hot	250/290	475/550	9/10

Dry Measures

Metric	Imperial
30 grams	1 ounce
45 grams	1½ ounces
55 grams	2 ounces
70 grams	2½ ounces
85 grams	3 ounces
100 grams	3½ ounces
110 grams	4 ounces
125 grams	4½ ounces
140 grams	5 ounces
280 grams	10 ounces
450 grams	16 ounces (1 pound)
500 grams	1 pound, 1½ ounces
700 grams	1½ pounds
800 grams	1¾ pounds
1 kilogram	2 pounds, 3 ounces
1.5 kilograms	3 pounds, 4½ ounces
2 kilograms	4 pounds, 6 ounces

Length

Metric	Imperial
0.5 cm	¼ inch
1 cm	½ inch
1.5 cm	¾ inch
2.5 cm	1 inch

Abbreviation

tsp	teaspoon
Tbsp	tablespoon
g	gram
kg	kilogram
ml	millilitre